Vicky Gets a Whipping
By Katie Nicole

The Following Fictional,
Erotic, Fantasy Story is meant
For Adults only, not children.

It is Erotica, Fantasy (NOT PORN)
Created for the soul enjoyment
Of an adult audience.

Enjoy!

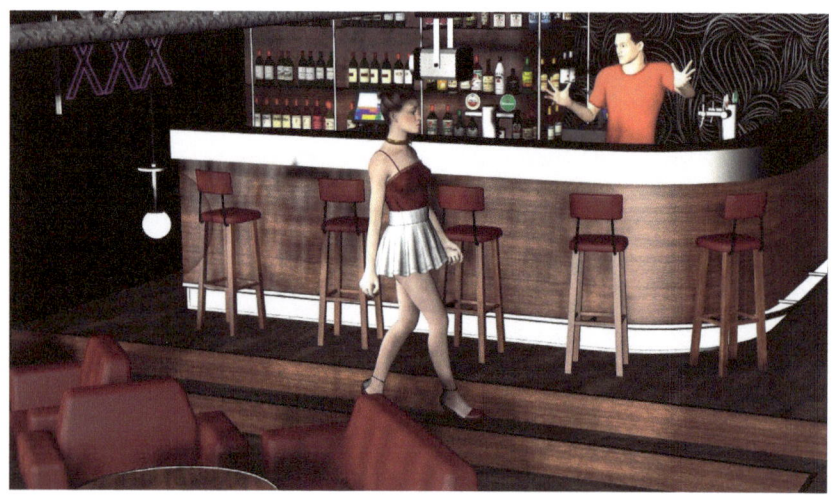

My name is Vicky. I am a young, submissive
Girl who works as a dancer at a Gentlemen's Club.

Today I was late once again getting to work.
Todd who is a bartender at the club, is
In love with me and has on many occasions
confessed that he would like to take me
Far away from this place and marry me.

When I came in late, he was very upset,
Because he knew the Club owner Bob would be
Furious with me and that I would be punished.

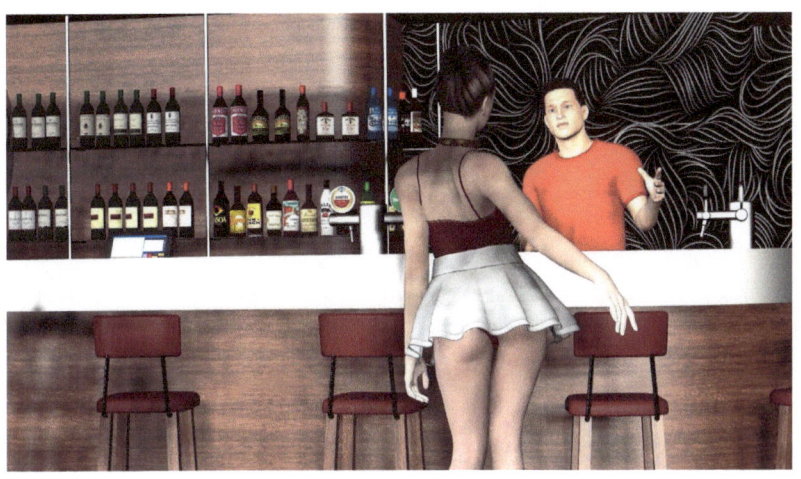

"Vicky Sweet Heart, why are you late again"

Asked Todd

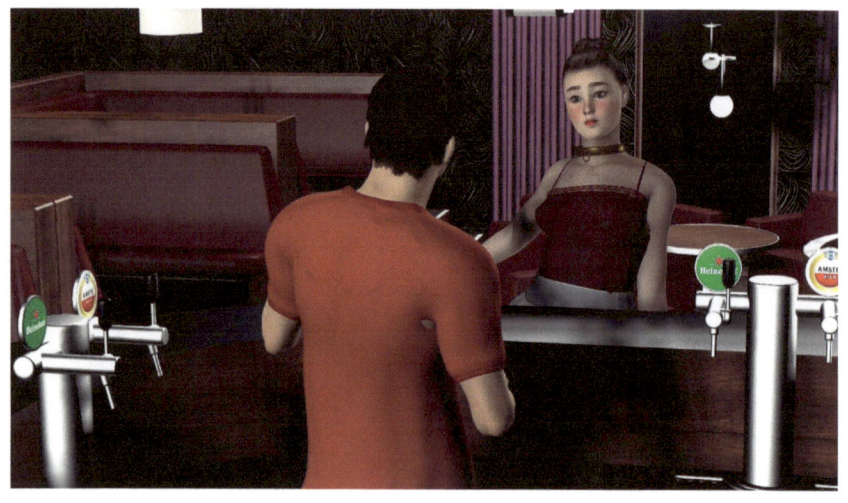

"I woke up late"

I replied

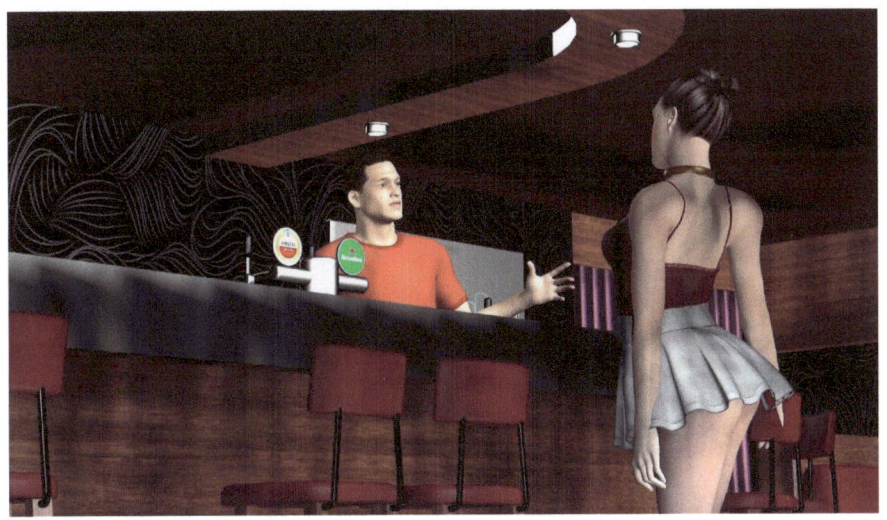

"Vicky, I love you, and I hate seeing what Bob
Does to you when you get in trouble"

Todd Confessed

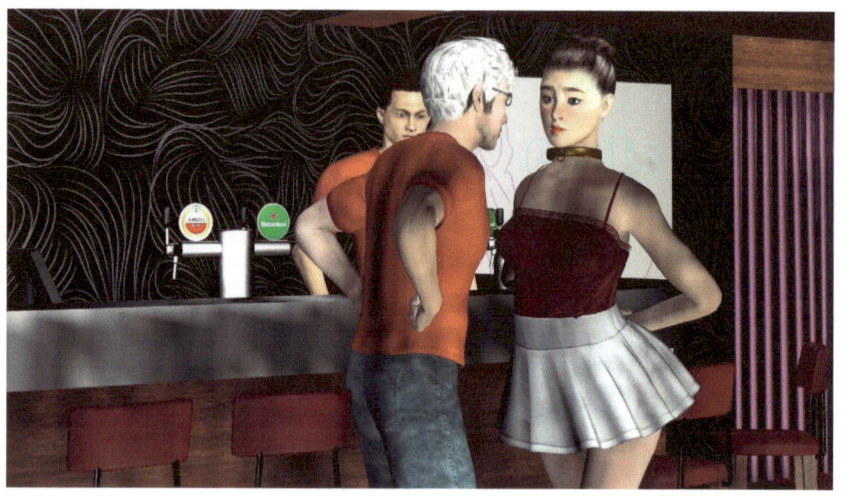

"You're in big trouble little lady, you know the Consequences for being late don't you Miss Vicky?"

Bob asked in a very angry voice.

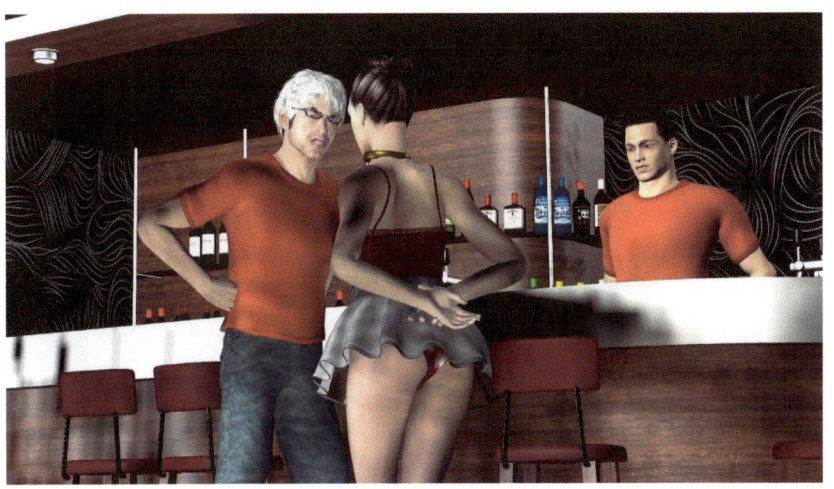

"Yes Sir, Sorry Sir"

I Replied

Then Bob said:

"After I'm finished with you in the
Dressing room, you are going to
Be publicly whipped in the club tonight"

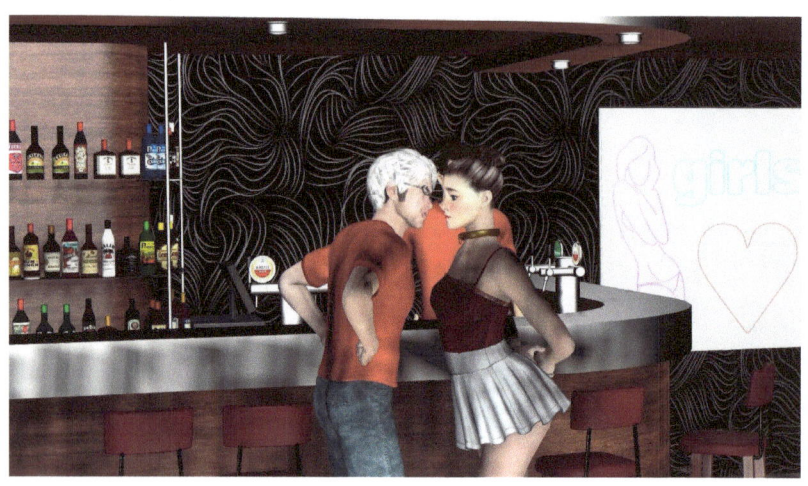

"Now go into the dressing room and wait for me"

Bob shouted

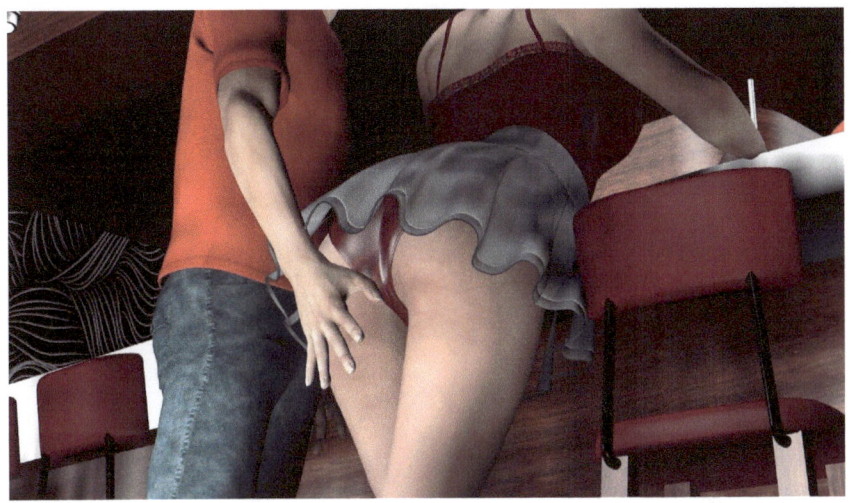

Then I went to bend over and give Todd a kiss before
I surrendered to the consequences of my lateness.
Bob swifty smacked my bottom hard.

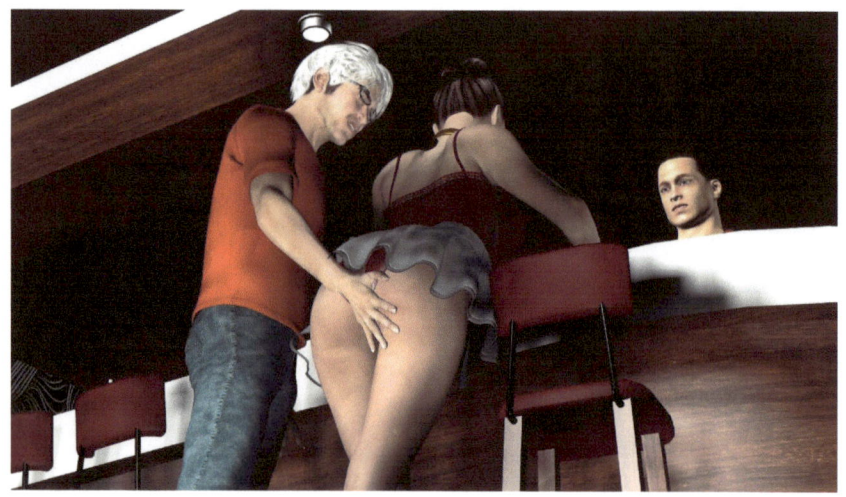

He grabbed me by my rear and said in a very stern voice:

"Go straight to the dressing room now!
Your butt mine now little lady"

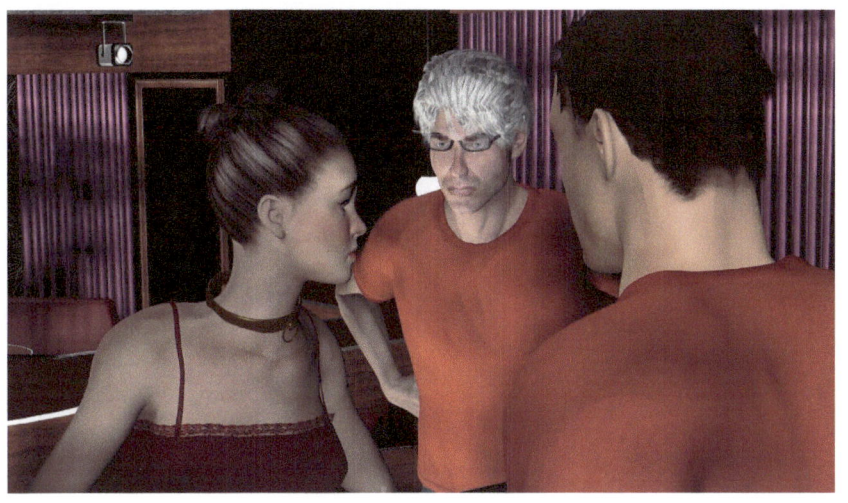

"Every second you delay Miss Vicky will result
In a more severe punishment"

Bob angrily said

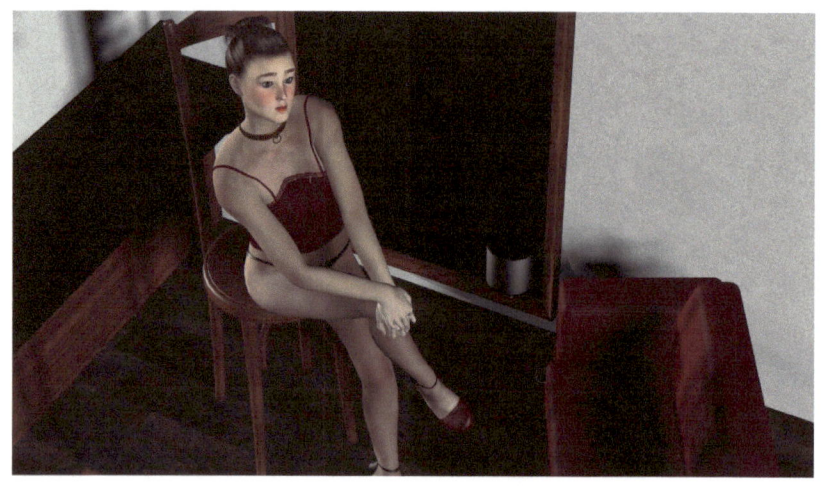

Nervously and anxiously I waited in the dressing room,
For Bob to come punish me. Flashbacks of
Waiting in my bedroom as a teenage girl for
My stepfather to come spank me, raced through my mind..

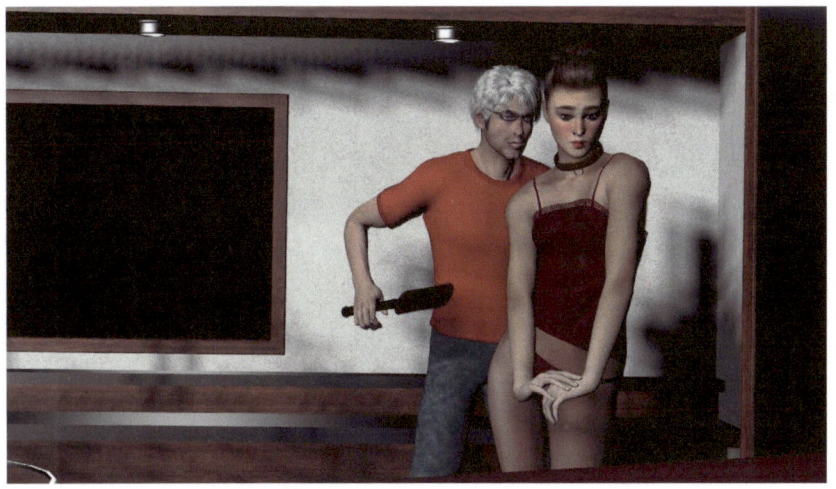

Bob arrived with his wicked black paddle in hand
And ordered me to bend over the couch.

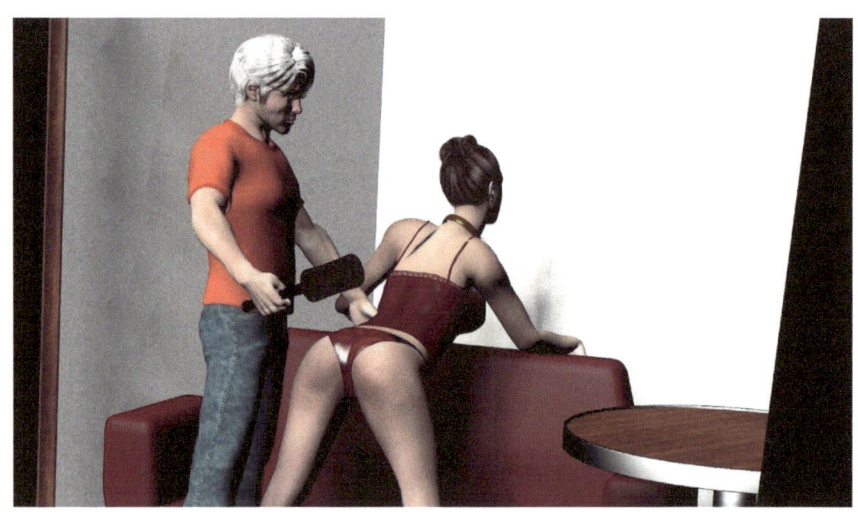

As he held me in place with one hand and
With the paddle in the other he said:

"Hold still, this is going to hurt"

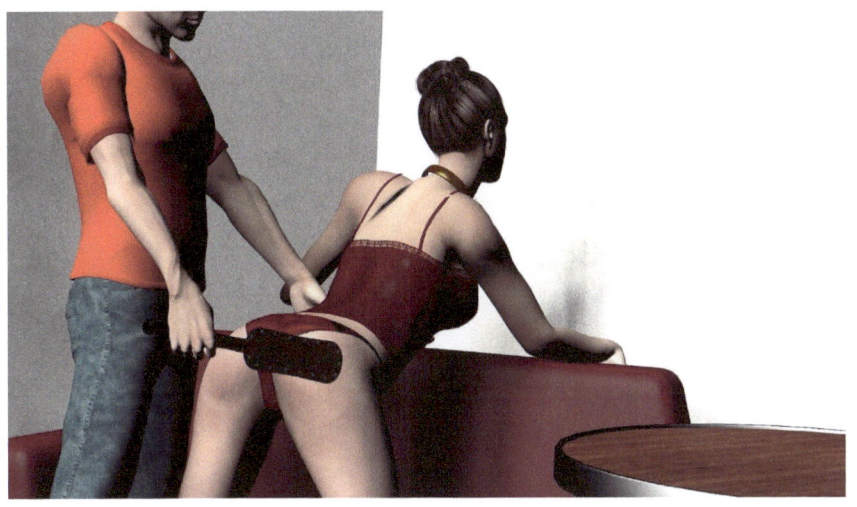

Bob forcefully applied the paddle to my tender bottom.
He spanked me good and hard, each stroke
Sending arousing vibrations all through my body
As I whimpered and moaned.

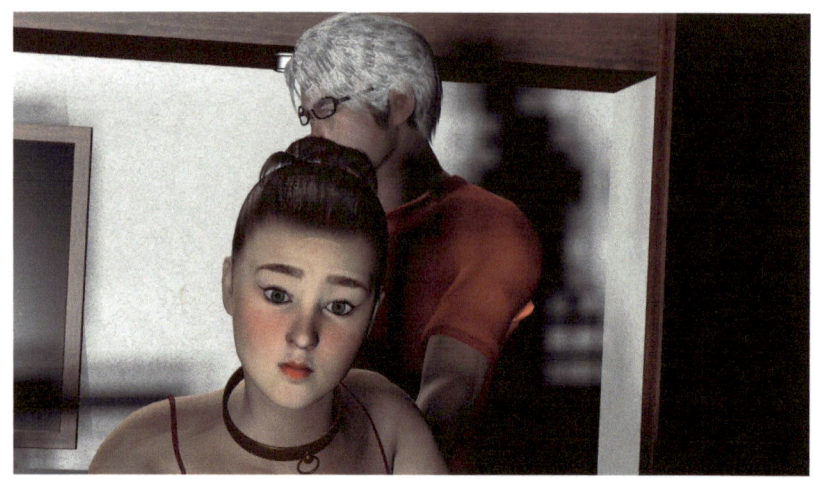

The sound of my bottom being firmly smacked
Echoed in the room as I trembled and shaked.

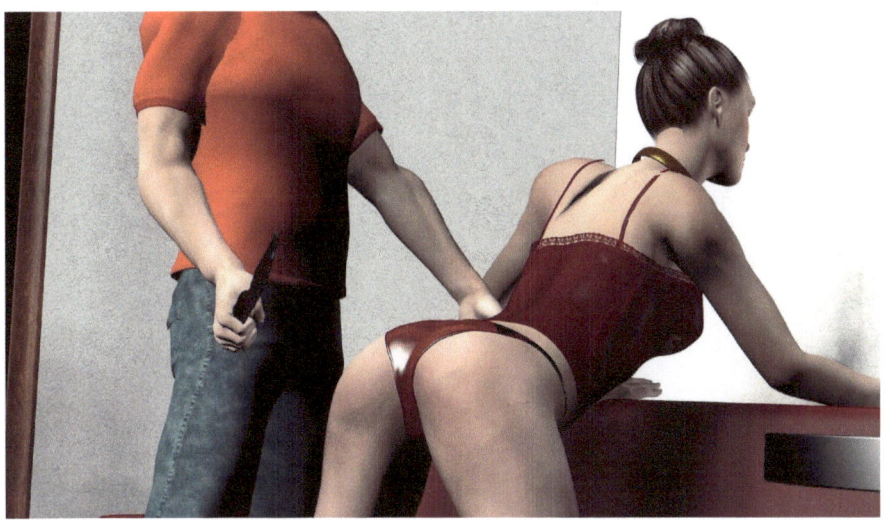

It was all I could do to hold still. Bob was very skilled with paddle
And knew just how to spank a girl to get the reaction he wanted.

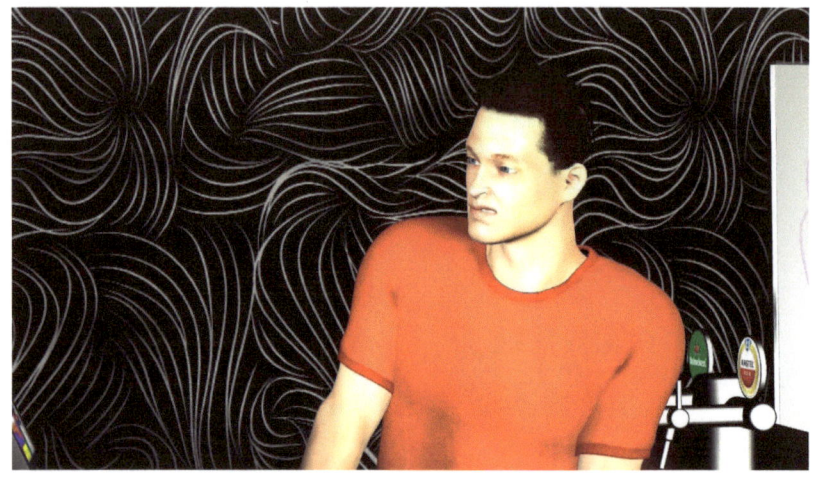

From the bar, Todd could hear me being spanked and
By the sound of my whimper and moans he knew
What it was doing to me.

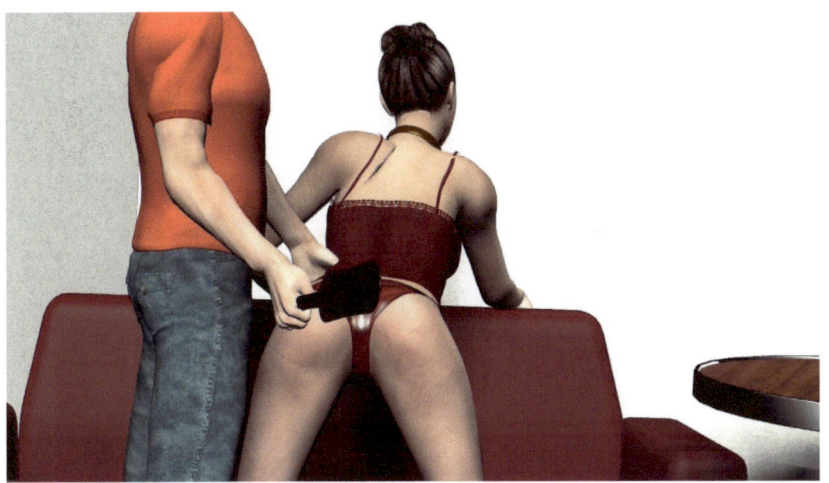

As the spanks kept coming I throbbed and pulsated inside.

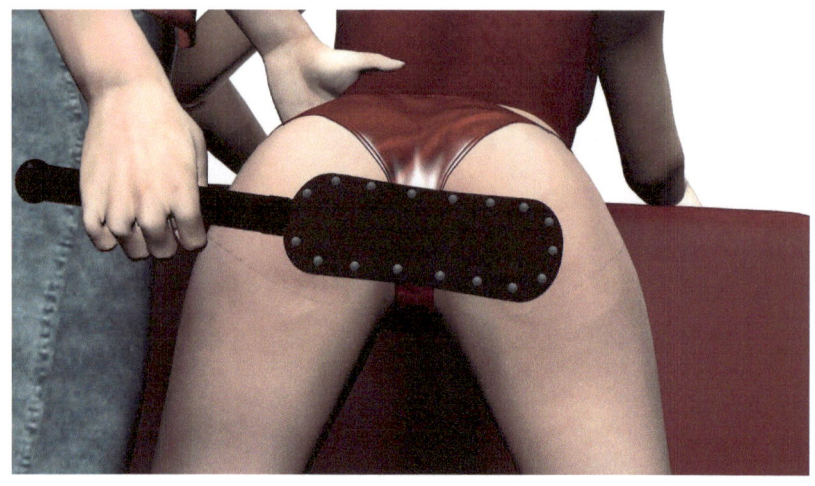

The wicked, black paddle applied to my
Tender sore bottom spanked me into
Uncontrollable convulsions.

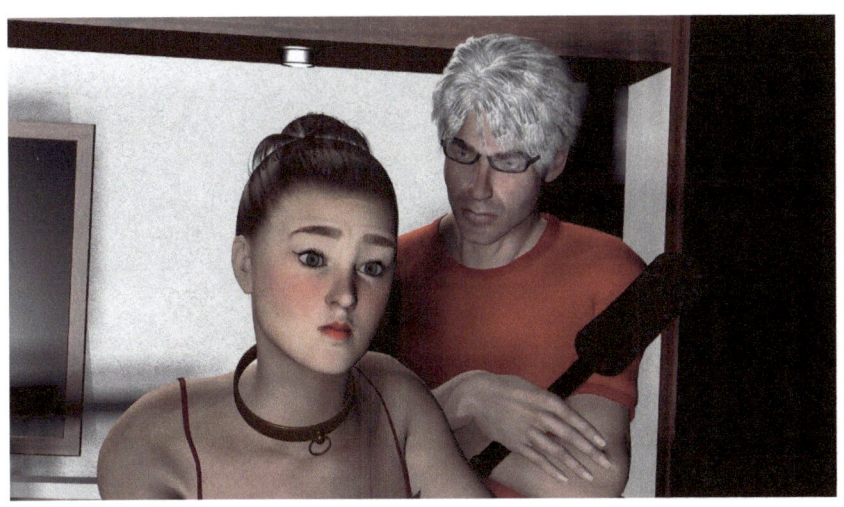

As I stood there trembling, Bob leaned over and said:

"Drop your panties little girl"

I knew what that meant.
Bob was a very, very well-endowed man.
I knew my bottom wasn't the
The only thing that was going
to be punished in that room.

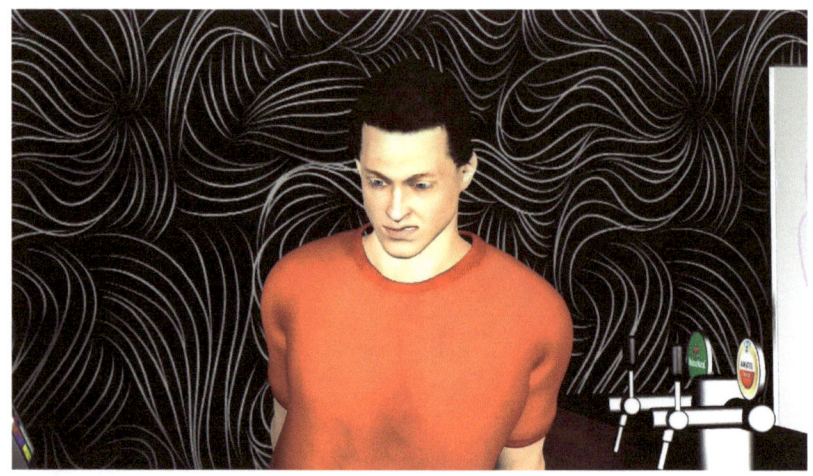

Poor Todd could hear that I was no longer being spanked
And knew by the sound my voice what Bob was doing to me now.

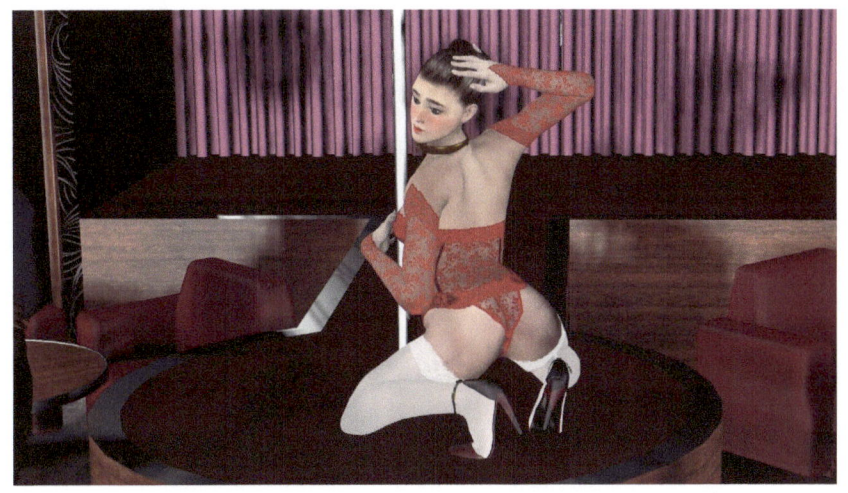

When the club opened I went out on stage
And did my dance routine.

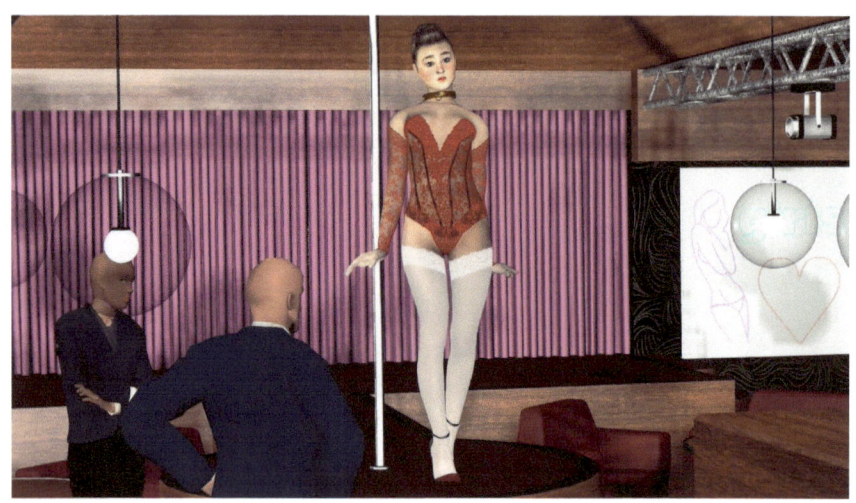

The men and women watched as I was on full display.

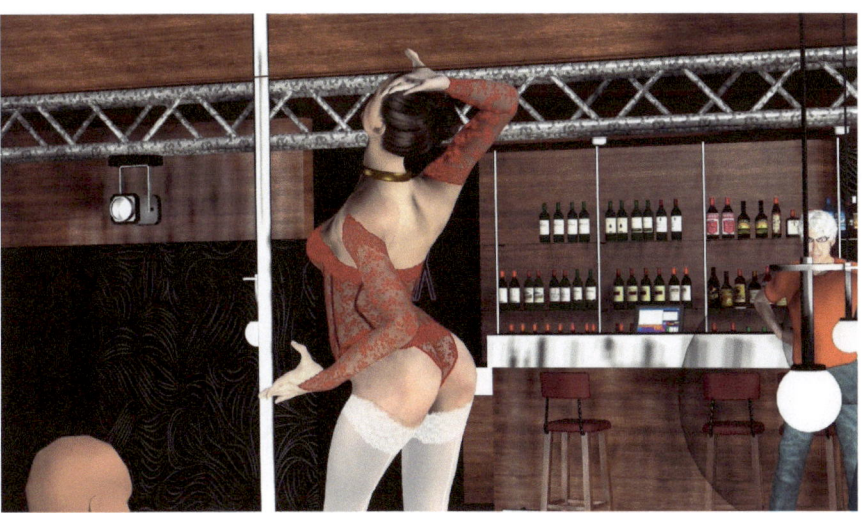

I could feel Bob and Todd watching me from the bar
As I danced along the stage with all eyes on me.

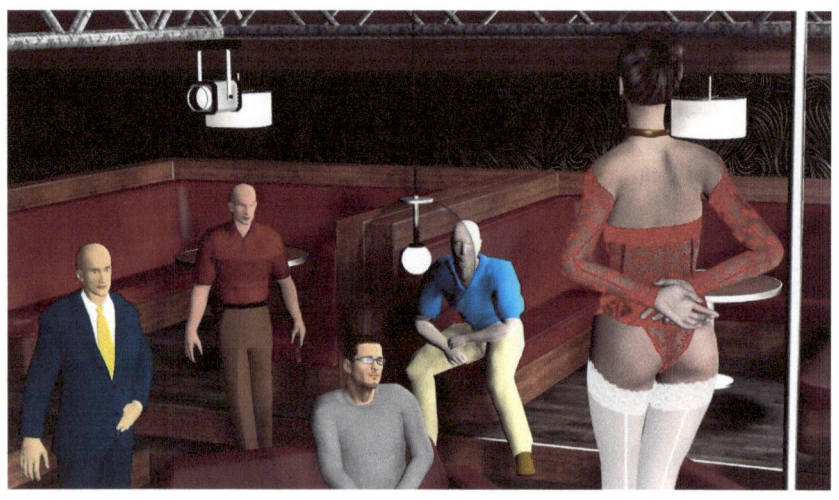

I looked over at the men and women watching me and knew
That I would have to soon be whipped in front of them.

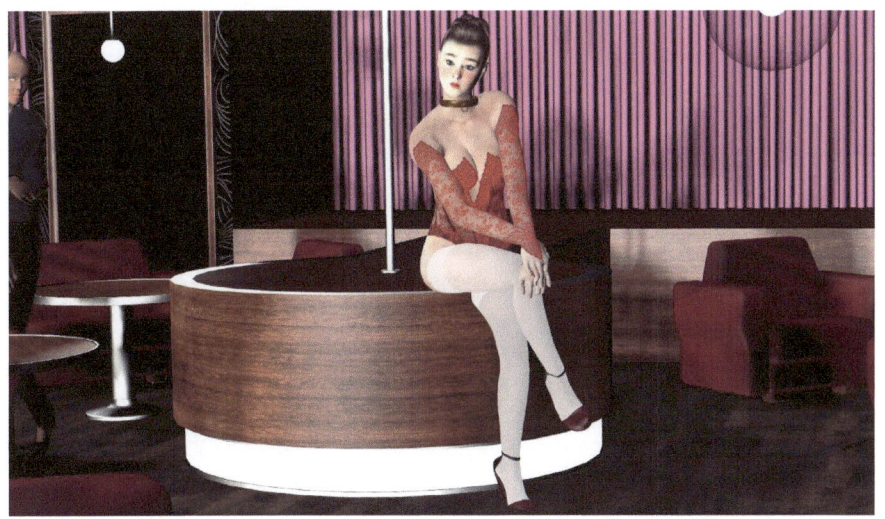

Finally I sat down on the stage and said:

"Ladies and Gentlemen, today I was a very bad girl
And I deserve a whipping. So I hereby acknowledge
That I willingly and deservedly submit to a public whipping"

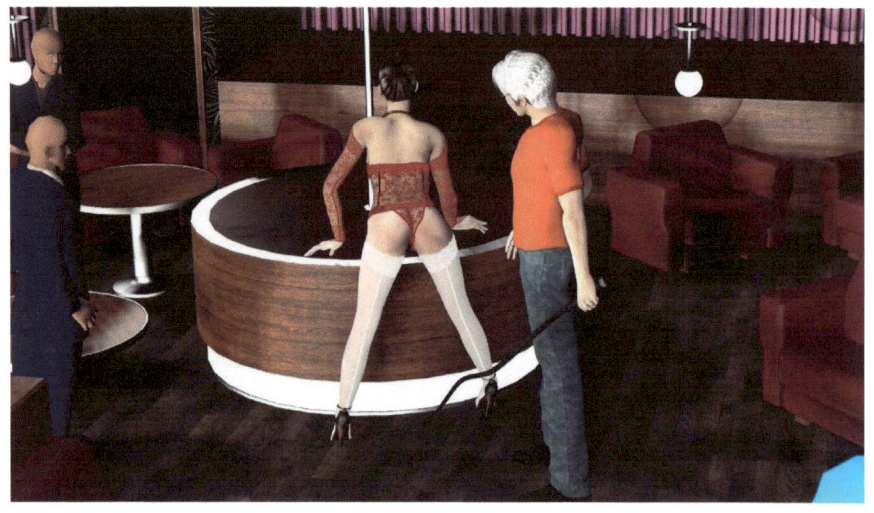

I bent over the stage as Bob brought out his
Thicked leather whip.

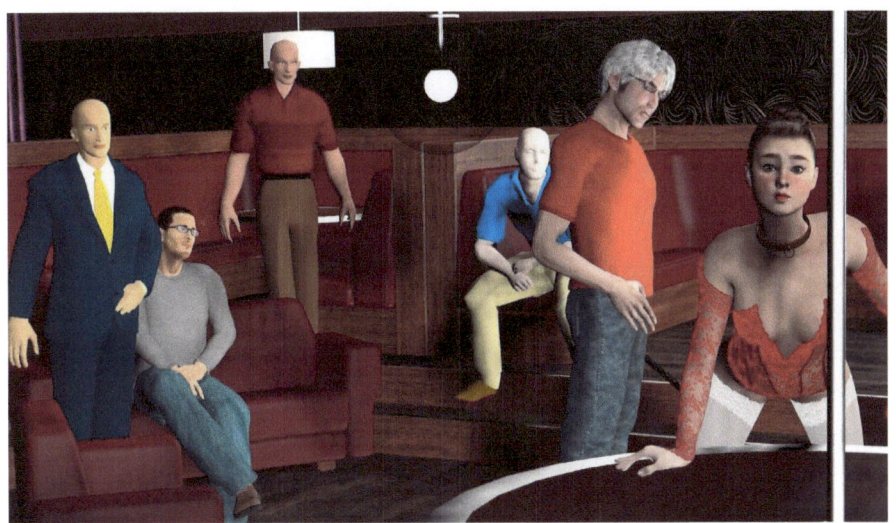

"Keep your bottom out and your back arched, If you Move from this position I will start your whipping all over again"

Bob said in a very stern, dominate, authoritative voice.

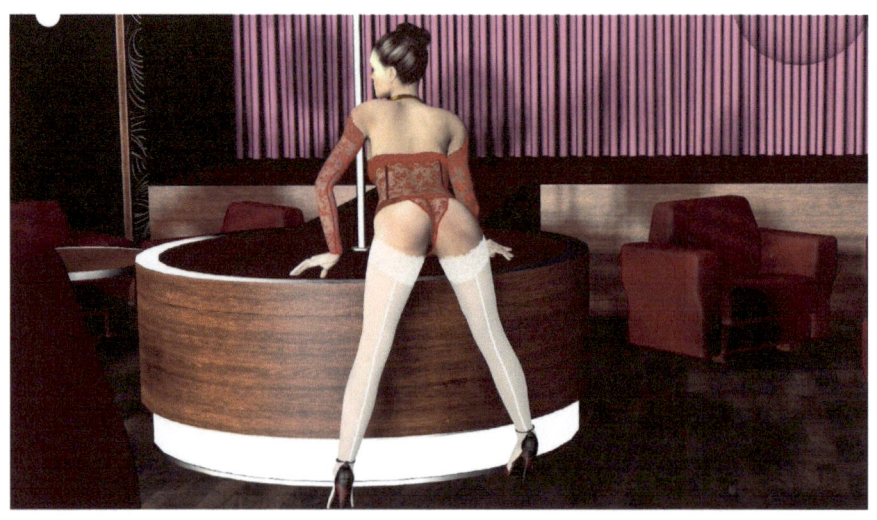

With my bottom up nice and high I waited for
My whipping to begin.

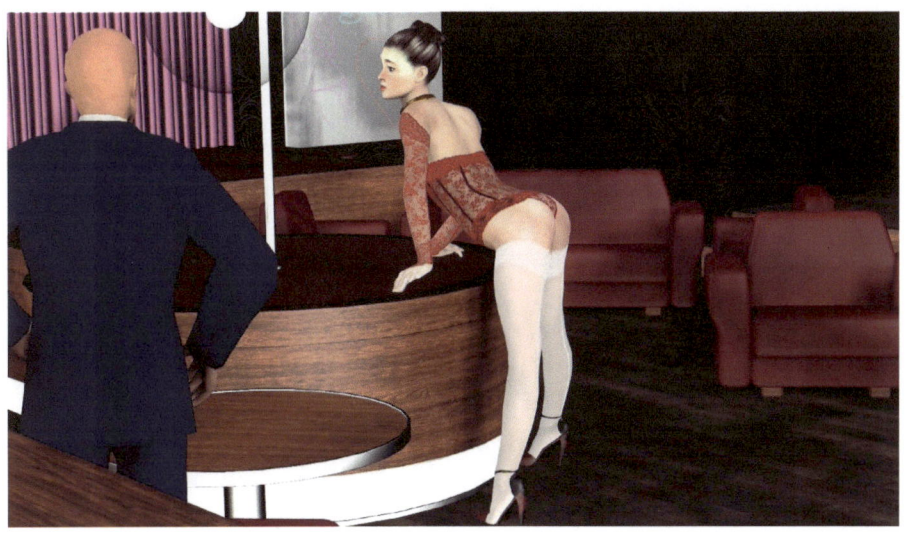

The men and women watched with great anticipation
To see me receive a thorough whipping.

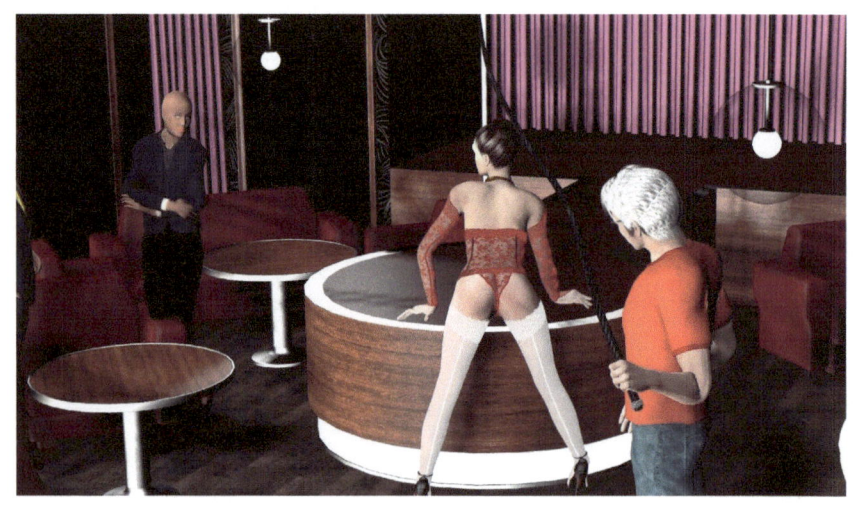

Bob pulled the whip back.

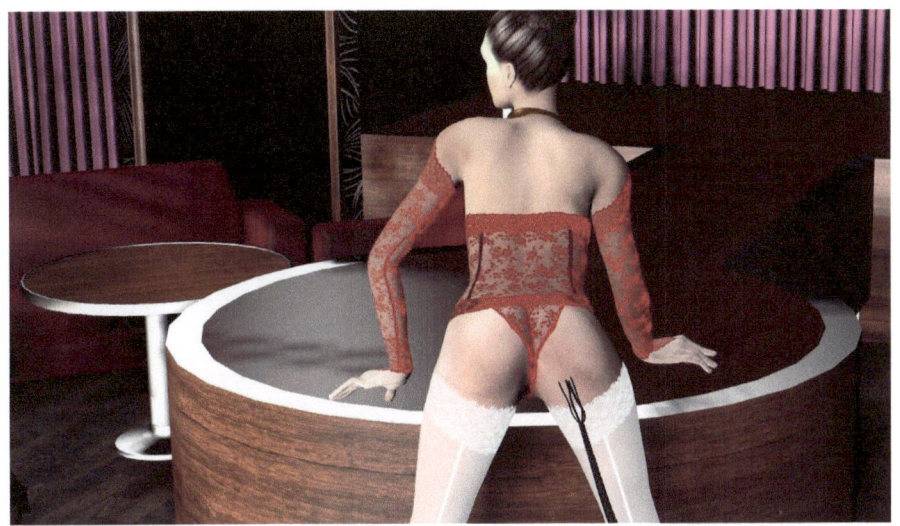

Then with a loud swoosh crack! The leather tongues
Of the whip licked my bottom as I let out a loud whimper.

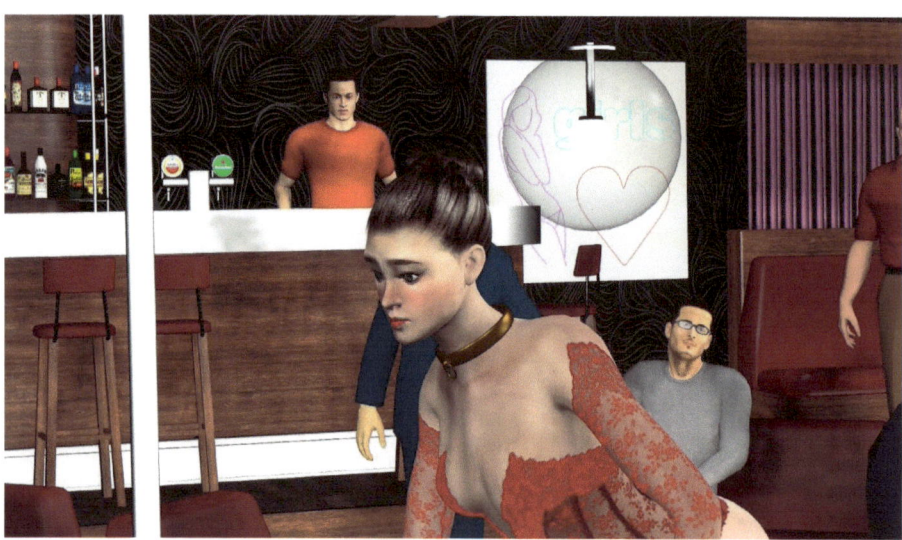

Todd watched in disgust as the girl he was in love with
Was viciously whipped by another man.

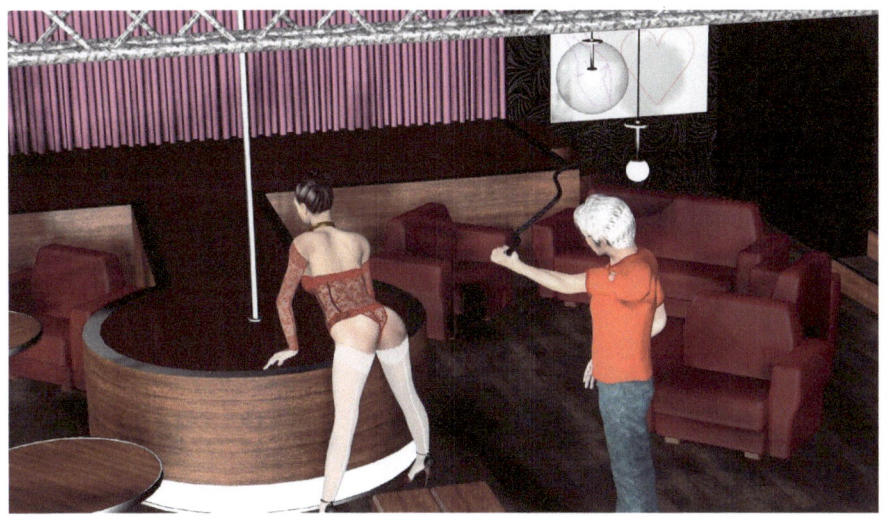

Lash after hot, wicked lash the whipping continued.

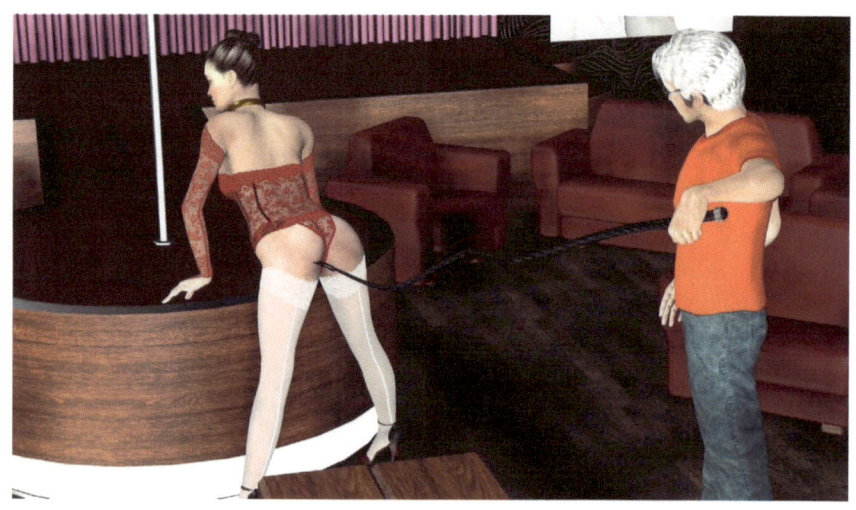

Bob was just as skilled with whip as he had been
With paddle knowing just where land each lick to
Get the desired arousing effect out of me.

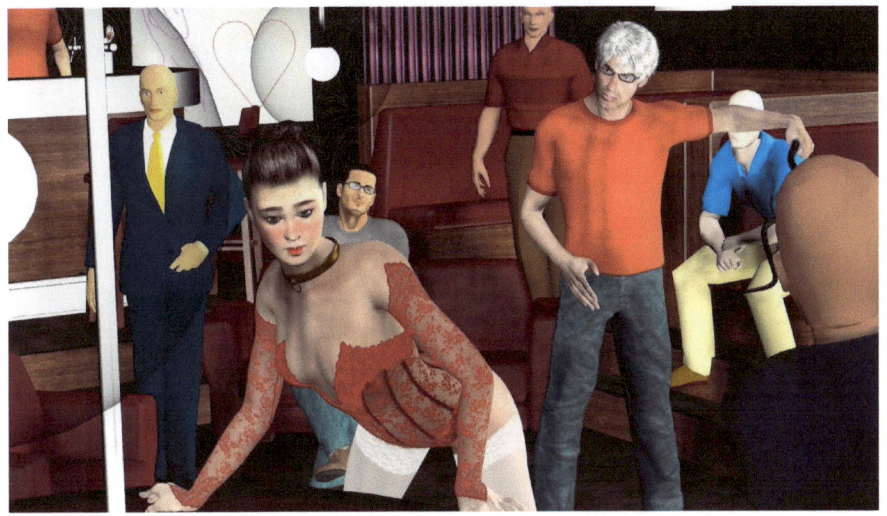

I was trembling and shaking all over again, but
This time in full view of an audience.

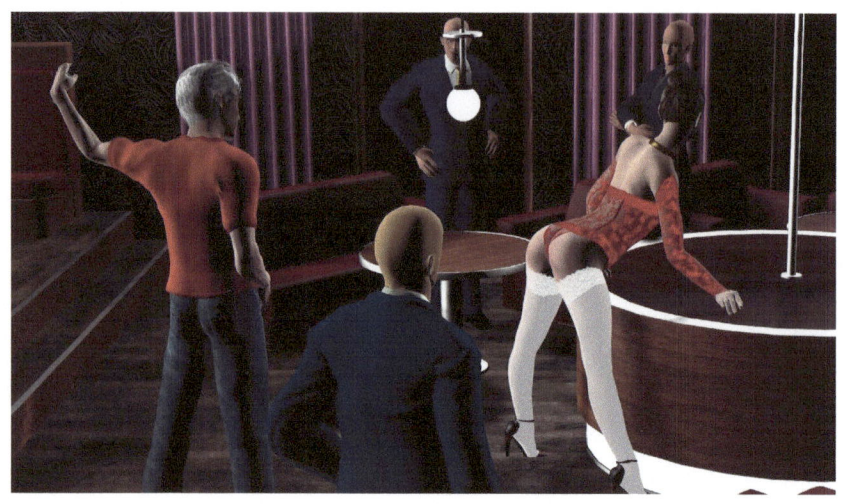

Swoosh Crack! Swoosh Crack!
The lashes came hot and fast.

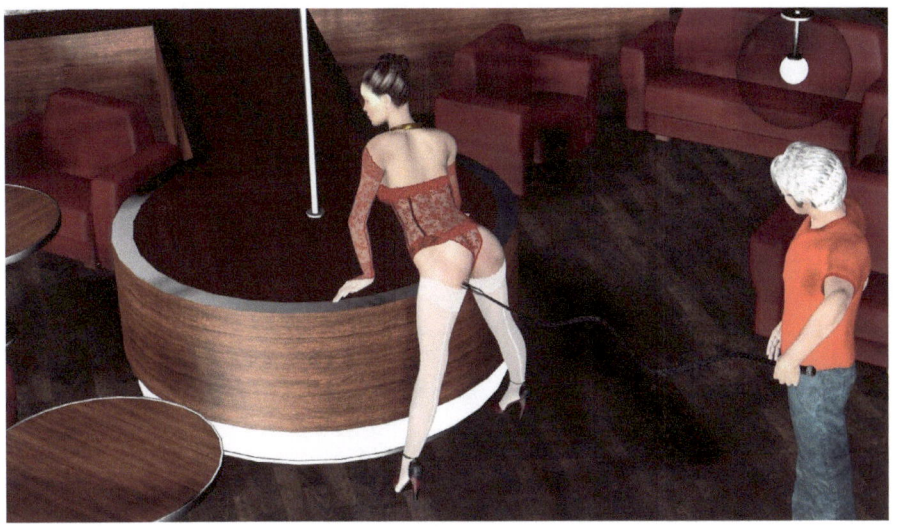

The sting of leather scorching my flesh as
I endorsed the my painful and arousing whipping.

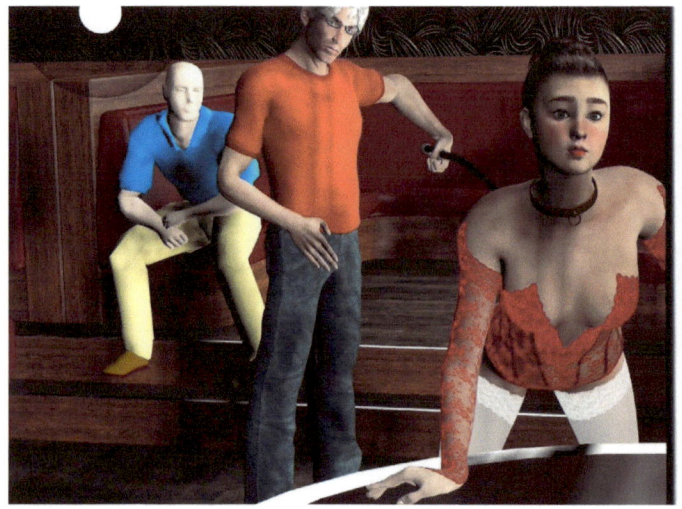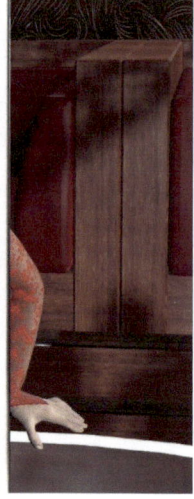

When the last lick was applied I was barely able to
Hold still any longer as I trembled and shaked.

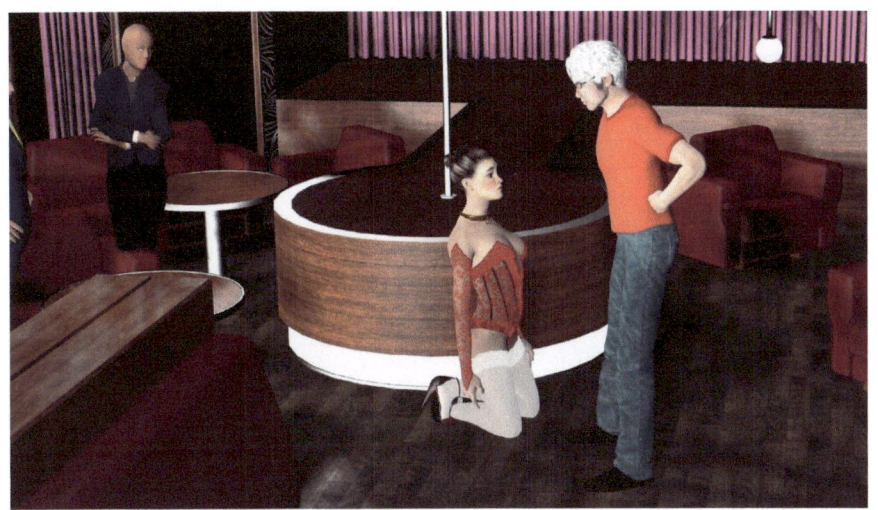

When it was all over I got down on my knees and
Thanked my punisher for my whipping.

The End.

Vicky Gets a Whipping
By Katie Nicole

Please check out the many other books
By Katie Nicole

Thank You for Reading.

www.ingramcontent.com/pod-product-compliance
Lightning Source LLC
Chambersburg PA
CBHW040334220526
45473CB00009B/2679